Alison Levendge

Three Tapping Teddies

Musical stories and chants for the very young

Kaye Umansky

with musical development by Helen MacGregor
and illustrations by Martin Pierce

A & C Black • London

First published 2000
A & C Black (Publishers) Ltd
35 Bedford Row
London WC1R 4JH

ISBN 0 7136 5118 0

All rights reserved.
No part of this publication may be reproduced or used in any form or by any means – photographic, electronic or mechanical, including photocopying, recording, taping or information storage and retrieval systems – without the prior permission in writing of the publishers.

Story text © Kaye Umansky
Music development
© Helen MacGregor
Illustrations © Martin Pierce
Cover artwork © Alex Ayliffe

Editors: Ana Sanderson and Sheena Roberts
Designer: Dorothy Moir
Printed in Great Britain by St Edmundsbury Press, Bury St Edmunds, Suffolk.

Material referred to in the text as photocopiable, may be photocopied for the teaching purposes specified in this book.

Contents

Little Red Riding Hood — page 3
Establishing the contrast between singing and speaking.

Brer Rabbit's talking house — 6
Exploring vocal tone.

The little house — 9
Exploring vocal and instrumental sound quality.

The meanest king — 12
Responding with movement to sound signals.

Pinocchio — 16
Moving in time to a steady beat.

Three tapping teddies — 18
Moving in time to a steady beat and controlling volume.

Goldilocks' tale — 22
Contrasting fast and slow, and contrasting pitch.

The magical musical box — 26
Contrasting ways of playing instruments, and controlling volume.

Squintum's   30
Selecting instrumental sound effects.

The big blue jeep and the little white trike   36
Telling a story with instrumental sounds.

Chicken Licken   40
Accumulating layers of sound.

The green wide-mouthed tree frog   44
Playing short rhythm patterns on instruments.

Please, Mr Noah   48
Accumulating vocal then instrumental rhythm patterns.

The aliens   52
Making up sound patterns; telling a story in sound.

Cinderella   56
Creating an instrumental accompaniment to a song.

Melody lines   62
All the melodies in staff notation with guitar chords.

Little Red Riding Hood

Young children need to experience the contrast between speaking and singing in order to discover their singing voices. In this story, Red Riding Hood's verses are sung to the tune of 'London Bridge', and the wolf's responses are chanted in gruff, speaking voices.

Red Riding Hood sings:
Granny, what big eyes you've got,
Eyes you've got, eyes you've got,
Granny, what big eyes you've got,
They're so funny.

Wolf chants gruffly:
All the better to see you with,
To see you with, to see you with,
All the better to see you with,
My sweet honey.

Red Riding Hood:
Granny, what big ears you've got ...
They're so funny.

Wolf:
All the better to hear you with ...
My sweet honey.

Red Riding Hood:
Granny, what big teeth you've got ...
They're so funny.

Wolf:
All the better to eat you with ...
My sweet honey.

Wolf: **ROAR!**
Red Riding Hood: **EEEEK!**

Little Red Riding Hood – activities

First things first
1. Play Mister Wolf.
2. Teach the Red Riding Hood song.
3. All say the Wolf's responses in gruff voices, finishing with a very loud roar and a yell!
4. Perform the whole story.

Mister Wolf

This game contrasts singing and speaking. The children ask in their singing voices how Mister Wolf is feeling; he replies in an appropriate speaking voice and the children match his tone.

Help the children pitch the song by playing it on chime bars E G and A.

1. Teach the children the song (the tune is based on the familiar playground chant), and the chanted responses opposite.
2. Choose a wolf and talk about his possible moods, eg happy, sad, sleepy ...
3. Start the game and repeat it until Mister Wolf answers 'hungry', showing claws and teeth. Whoever sits most still and silent becomes the next Mister Wolf.

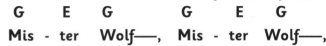

All sing

G	E	G		G	E	G
Mis	- ter	Wolf—	,	Mis	- ter	Wolf—,

G	E	A	G	E	G	E	G
How	are you	feel	-	ing,	Mis	- ter	Wolf—?

Mister Wolf chants in a grumpy tone
I'm feeling grumpy, I'm feeling grumpy.

All chant, copying Mister Wolf's tone
**Mis - ter Wolf,   Mis - ter Wolf,
He's feeling grum - py, Mis - ter Wolf.**

Brer Rabbit's talking house

The focus is on exploring tones of voice in this story which features a wolf who tries to disguise his voice to sound like a house.

One day, when everyone was out, sneaky old Brer Wolf crept on over to Brer Rabbit's house and hid inside. Later that morning, Brer Rabbit came home from a walk and noticed that everything was very still. The door was open a crack. Funny. His wife always shut the door tight.

He peeped in at the windows and he listened down the chimney. But he couldn't see or hear a thing.

Absolute silence.

Brer Rabbit said to himself (suspiciously):

**Hidin' up the chimney?
Underneath the bed?
Waitin' by the window?
Crouchin' in the shed?**

**Somebody is in there,
Quiet as can be,
Only thing I know is –
Sure ain't me!**

Now, Brer Rabbit was good at tricks. He thought and he thought. He knew somebody was hiding in his house – but who? He certainly didn't want to go inside to find out. It wasn't long before he came up with a clever idea. He went a little way from the house and shouted (loudly and cheerfully):

**Hey there, house!
Nice, fine day.
How you doin'?
All okay?**

The house didn't answer. Inside, behind the door, Brer Wolf could hardly believe his ears. What was Brer Rabbit doing, talking to his house? He peeped through the

crack in the door, but couldn't see a thing. Brer Rabbit called again (louder):

**Hey there house!
Ain't you talkin'?
What you done
While I been walkin'?**

Silence from the house. Brer Wolf was beginning to feel quite nervous. Especially when Brer Rabbit called out again (crossly):

**Hey there, house!
You feel sick?
Speak up now
And make it quick!**

Brer Wolf thought he had better do something before Brer Rabbit got suspicious. But how did a talking house sound? He took a deep breath, made his voice as hoarse as he could, and shouted:

HEY YOURSELF!

Brer Rabbit grinned to himself. Then he shouted (curiously):

**Hey there, house!
Why you croakin'?
Guess your chimney
Must be smokin'!**

Brer Wolf cleared his throat and shouted again, this time in his own voice:

HEY YOURSELF!

Brer Rabbit laughed so much he couldn't stand up straight.

'Hey, Brer Wolf!' he shouted. 'You've got some practising to do if you want to sound like a house!'

And, feeling rather silly, Brer Wolf slunk away.

Brer Rabbit's talking house – activities

First things first
Tell the story to the children, emphasising the changes in vocal tone in Brer Rabbit's chants and the Wolf's responses.

Extension 1
1. Play Talking house.
2. Retell the story with everyone joining in with Brer Rabbit's last two chants and with Brer Wolf's responses.

Extension 2
1. Teach all the chants and practise saying them in the dramatic style indicated: suspiciously, cheerfully, crossly …
2. Choose a child to be Brer Wolf, and tell the story again. You might use the home corner or a large cardboard box for Brer Wolf to hide in.

Talking house

Play this game to encourage the children to explore their voices.

1. Choose a child to be Brer Rabbit. He stands facing away from the group and chants (with your help to begin with):

> Hey there, house!
> You feel sick?
> Speak up now and
> Make it quick!

2. Point to a child in the group to be Brer Wolf. This child replies in a voice disguised to sound like a talking house and says:

 **HEY YOURSELF!**

3. Brer Rabbit turns round and points to the child he thinks is Brer Wolf. This time Brer Rabbit chants:

> Hey there, house!
> Why you croakin'?
> Guess your chimney
> Must be smokin'!

The real Brer Wolf says, 'Hey yourself' in his or her own voice and so is revealed, and becomes the next Brer Rabbit.

The little house

The children explore sound quality in the different voices for Mrs Mouse, Mr Frog and Big Brown Bear.

Once, a big, clay jar rolled off the back of a cart that was going to market. It came to rest in the grass by the side of the road. By and by, Mrs Mouse came along.

 (MRS MOUSE SOUNDS)

She looked at the jar and she said in her high, squeaky little voice:

**Little house, little house,
Who lives in the little house?**

Nobody answered, so Mrs Mouse moved in and began to live there.

By and by, Mr Frog came hopping along.

 (MR FROG SOUNDS)

He looked at the jar and he said in his croaky voice:

**Little house, little house,
Who lives in the little house?**

And he heard a high, squeaky little voice say:

**Mrs Mouse, Mrs Mouse,
I live in the little house.
But who are you?**

And Mr Frog said, 'Mr Frog is my name, and I'm very pleased to meet you.'

Mrs Mouse replied, 'Come in, Mr Frog, and we'll live together.

So Mrs Mouse and Mr Frog lived happily together in the little house.

By and by, Big Brown Bear came along the road.

 (BIG BROWN BEAR SOUNDS)

He saw the little house, and in his big, deep, gruff voice he said:

**Little house, little house,
Who lives in the little house?**

And he heard a high, squeaky voice and a croaky voice reply:

**Mr Frog and Mrs Mouse,
We live in the little house.
But who are you?**

And Big Brown Bear said, 'Big Brown Bear is my name, and I'm going to squash you FLAT!'

And he sat on the little house and squashed it all flat!

(SQUASHING SOUND)

And that was the end of the little house. But it wasn't the end of Mr Frog and Mrs Mouse. They got out just in time and went to live on a lily pad where it was much, much safer.

The little house – activities

First things first
1. Tell the story, representing the different characters with your own voice.
2. Perform the chants as a class, emphasising the difference between the voices.
3. Confident individuals may take turns acting out the story and saying the chants.

Extension
1. Play Who's in the house?

2. Choose individuals or small groups of children to play the mouse, frog and bear instruments you selected for the game, while you tell the story and everyone else joins in with the chants.
3. Play the instruments at the cue for each animal's arrival.
4. Find a sound to play for the squashing of the little house.

Who's in the house?

This game familiarises children with the sound qualities of different instruments.

1. As a class, discuss and choose three different percussion instruments to represent the voices of the mouse, frog and bear.
2. Draw each on a picture card, eg

3. Play each instrument in turn then hide them all behind a screen.
4. Everyone chants:

> Little house, little house,
> Who lives in the little house?

Choose one child to select and play one of the hidden instruments.
5. Everyone else listens to the answer. Depending on what the child can manage, this might be a single sound or may be the rhythm of the chant words, eg

Mis - ses Mouse,   Mis - ses Mouse,

I live in the   lit - tle house.

6. The listeners identify the animal they think they heard by pointing to its picture.
7. Two children can play two of the three instruments simultaneously. Can the listeners identify both animals?
8. Vary the instruments and animals to increase the children's experience of sounds.

The meanest king

The children develop their responses to sound signals by dancing when they hear the magic rattle and stopping when it stops. There are instrumental sound effects to make up, and two songs to sing: the first is sung to the tune of 'Twinkle, twinkle little star', the second to 'What shall we do with the drunken sailor?'

Once upon a time there lived the meanest king. He sat on his throne all day long, growling and stamping his feet and shouting at everyone. He had some very mean guards who snarled and hissed and cracked their whips,

CRACK!

The meanest king never smiled or laughed or danced. He hated his people to be happy. He made them work in the hot sun all day. If they wanted to stop for a rest or a drink, he would wave his fists and shout:

NO!

Now, up in the sky there flew a little sparrow.

(FLYING SOUND EFFECT)

She had been watching the king, and saw how meanly he had been treating his people. She thought it was time to teach him a lesson. She flew up, up, up into the sky ...

(FLYING UP SOUND EFFECT)

... and from a secret place behind the clouds, she took a magic rattle. The rattle had special power. It could make things invisible!

And this is what the sparrow sang (to the tune of 'Twinkle, twinkle, little star'):

**Magic rattle, cast your spell,
Where I go, no one can tell.
They won't see me when I fly,
They won't know I'm passing by.
Magic rattle, cast your spell,
Where I go, no one can tell.**

Then she took the magic rattle, and as she flew down, down ...

(FLYING DOWN SOUND EFFECT)

... down to earth, she became invisible.

The people were working in the fields in the hot sun. The invisible sparrow flew over them, shaking the rattle. When the people heard the sound, they stopped working and began to laugh and sing and dance. They just couldn't help themselves. Even the mean guards joined in! (Sing to the tune of 'What shall we do with the drunken sailor?')

**What shall we do when we hear the rattle?
What shall we do when we hear the rattle?
What shall we do when we hear the rattle?
Dance and sing all morning!**
   (Play rattle, sing and dance)
**Dance to the magic rattle,
Dance to the magic rattle,
Dance to the magic rattle,
Dance and sing all morning!**
   (Continue to play and dance)

The meanest king heard the singing! He came out of his palace and saw everyone laughing and dancing. He shouted:

STOP! (Hold the rattle still)

The sparrow stopped playing. Everyone went silent.

The meanest king looked at his fields. And he roared a huge roar.

ROARRRRRRRR!

The people were terrified! But the invisible sparrow just flew up, up, up, over the king's head, shaking the magic rattle.

(RATTLE AND
FLYING UP SOUND EFFECT)

(Continue to play the rattle.) And a wonderful thing happened. The king smiled. Then he laughed.

Then he danced. He smiled and laughed and danced for three days and nights – and everyone else joined in! (Everyone sings and dances to the rattle.)

Dance to the magic rattle ...

Finally, the rattle stopped and everyone fell to the ground. The king was laughing so much, it was ages before he got his breath back. But when he did, he said, 'I've been a very mean king. I'm really very sorry, and I promise to be a kind, jolly king from now on.'

And the people shouted:

HOORAY FOR THE KING!

And the sparrow flew away, taking her magic rattle with her.

(FLYING SOUND EFFECT)

The meanest king – activities

First things first
1. Play Magic rattle.
2. Tell the story and cue the dancing by playing the rattle as directed in the story.

Extension 1
1. Play a glockenspiel to represent the sparrow's flight. Run a beater back and forth across the middle bars for normal flight. When she flies up, run the beater across the bars from bottom (longest bar) to top. Reverse this when she flies down.
2. Make up an accompaniment of magical sounds for the first song – shake a bell tree, tap a triangle gently, play wind chimes.
3. Tell the story again with children acting the parts of the sparrow, guards, king and people.

Extension 2
Play Magic signals.

Magic rattle

1. You need a rattle or maraca, and a clear space in which the children can dance.
2. Explain to the children that when they hear the rattle they may move, when the rattle is silent, they must stand very still.
3. Begin playing very quietly – the children respond with little jiggles or even just wiggling fingers. Play more loudly and the children respond with more energetic dancing.

Magic signals

Instrumental sounds give the signals for different body actions in this lively game.
1. Choose three contrasting instruments, eg drum, bell, shaker.
2. Choose body actions for each sound, eg

drum   bell   shaker

3. Rehearse this new version of the song:

What shall we do when we hear the music?
What shall we do when we hear the music?
What shall we do when we hear the music?
What shall we do all morning?

4. Choose one child, the sparrow, to play one of the instruments, eg the bell. The other children then sing and move appropriately for the chorus:

> Nod to the magic bell,
> Nod to the magic bell,
> Nod to the magic bell,
> Nod our heads all morning.

5. Repeat the game with a new sparrow.
6. Make the game more challenging – choose three similar-sounding instruments, eg Indian bells, triangle, cymbal.

Pinocchio

Sing this action song to the tune of Polly put the kettle on. It develops the ability to coordinate moving in time to a steady beat.

My name is Pinocchio,
I am in a puppet show,
I can move my wooden arm,
It goes like this.
Here is what my arm can do,
See if you can do it too,
Here is what my arm can do,
It goes like this.

My name is Pinocchio,
I am in a puppet show,
I can move my other arm,
It goes like this.
Here is what my arm can do,
See if you can do it too,
Here is what my arm can do,
It goes like this.

My name is Pinocchio,
I am in a puppet show,
I can move my wooden leg,
It goes like this.
Here is what my leg can do ...

My name is Pinocchio,
I am in a puppet show,
I can move my other leg,
It goes like this.
Here is what my leg can do ...

My name is Pinocchio,
I am in a puppet show,
I can dance around the room,
I dance like this.
Here's the dance that I can do,
See if you can do it too,
Here's the dance that I can do,
It goes like this.

Pinocchio - activities

First things first

1. Before singing the song, encourage the children to try out puppet-like actions. Show them the movements of a simple wooden string puppet.
2. Sing the song quite slowly and move the appropriate part of the body in time to the beat, which corresponds with each syllable:

   My name is Pi - noc - chi - o ...

3. In the final verse, the children can devise their own individual dance movements.

Extension 1
Ask individual children to suggest extra verses and then demonstrate matching movements for the class to copy, eg

   I can nod my wooden head ...

Extension 2
Play Pinocchio's band.

Pinocchio's band

Sing this instrumental version of Pinocchio's song. The children have already practised the physical coordination of moving their bodies in time to a steady beat. Now they transfer the skill to playing, or miming playing, a percussion instrument.

1. The children stand in a circle. Choose a child to be Pinocchio and to stand in the centre with as many of these instruments as you have available: woodblock and beater, hand drum, drum and stick, agogo bells and stick, claves, ankle or wrist bells, coconut shells, tambourine, guiro and stick, jingle bells. Ask the child to choose then play an instrument on the beat as you sing the song.

My   name is   Pi - noc - chi - o,
I   am   in   a   mu - sic show,
I   can play a   ma - gic drum, it
Goes   like   this.
Here is   what my   drum can do,
See if   you can   do   it   too,
Dum dum dum dum   dum dum dum, it
Goes   like   this.

2. Repeat the song all the way through to the sound words 'dum dum dum ...' Mime playing the drum, copying the solo child.
3. Repeat. The children take turns to be Pinocchio and choose an instrument.
4. Confident children can sing the verse as a solo, everyone joining in with the repeat.

Three tapping teddies

Step in time to this chant - quietly, more loudly, then very loudly.

Leader: **Are you ready?** Are you steady? Here's a tiny tapping teddy!
All: **Tap,** tap, tap, tap. Tiny tapping teddy! L: **Are you ready?** Are you steady? Here's a bigger tapping teddy!
All: **Tap,** tap, tap, tap. Bigger tapping teddy! L: **Are you ready?** Are you steady? Here's a huge tapping teddy!
All: **Tap,** tap, tap, tap. Huge tapping teddy!

Three tapping teddies – activities

First things first
Teach the chant with these movements.
1. Leader: walk your feet – left right, left right – throughout the chant. (The teddy paws above the words indicate the beat.) Step quietly for the tiny teddy, more loudly for the bigger teddy, and loudly for the huge teddy.
2. The children join in for the responses (but you need not discourage them from joining in throughout – younger children will anyway). Encourage the children to match your dynamic (quiet, medium, loud).

Extension 1
Play Paws.

Extension 2
1. When they know the chant well, some children may like to be leader.

Extension 3
Change the chant to include different vocal or body sounds, eg

> Are you ready, are you steady?
> Here's a tiny swimming teddy.
> Swish swish swish swish,
> Tiny swimming teddy.
>   Swish swish …

Try clapping, squeaking, snoring, and so on.

Paws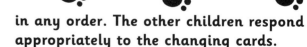

This game helps the children refine contrast between dynamics. You will need enlarged photocopies of the paw cards opposite.

1. Show the children all three cards and practise stepping at the appropriate dynamic for each – quietly for the small paws, very loudly for the biggest. You may like to set a beat for the children by saying 'tap tap tap tap …' as in the chant.
2. Now show one card. Can the children, or confident individuals, remember at which dynamic to step?
3. Ask one child to hold up each card in turn in any order. The other children respond appropriately to the changing cards.

Extension
1. Transfer the game to percussion. Tap small drums, tambours, woodblocks, sticks, or yoghurt pots, aiming for a clear contrast in dynamic and using the cards to signal the changes.
2. In pairs or small groups, the children can explore more instruments. They may find that it is easier to make clearer dynamic contrasts on some instruments than on others. Which are these?

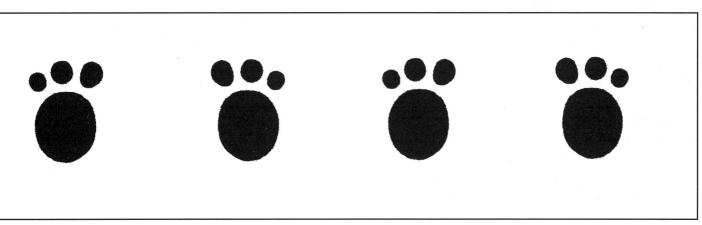
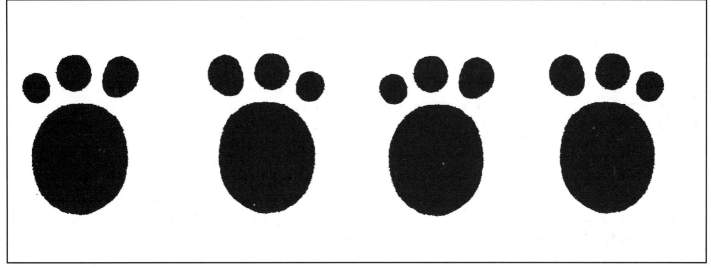

pulse
fast/slow tempo

Goldilocks' tale

Contrast large and small actions, fast and slow actions, and add instruments to this chant.

I don't like eating from
    a great big bowl,
A great big bowl,
    a great big bowl.
I don't like eating from
    a middle-sized bowl.
The small one's right for me.

I don't like sitting in
    a great big chair,
A great big chair,
    a great big chair.
I don't like sitting in
    a middle-sized chair.
The small one's right for me.

I don't like sleeping in
    a great big bed,
A great big bed,
    a great big bed.
I don't like sleeping in
    a middle-sized bed.
The small one's right for me.
(Place head on hands and sleep.)

BUT THE BEARS HAVE COME HOME!
(Tap knees quickly and lightly, or play instruments.)

I jump through the window
    and I run run run,
I run run run,
    and I run run run,
I jump through the window
    and I run run run,
Till I get to my own little **HOUSE!**
('Slam door' action – all stop playing.)

(Slowly and sleepily stretch, or play instruments.)

I get home safe and make
    a great big yawn,
A great big yawn,
    a great big yawn.
There are no more bears
    so I climb the stairs,
As tired as tired can be.
(Go to sleep.)

Goldilocks' tale – activities

First things first
1. Chant the story to the children, encouraging them to join in with actions which indicate the size of the bowls, chairs and beds. Let them pick up the words as they go along.
2. At the running section, everyone taps knees with left and right hands as fast as each can.
3. On 'HOUSE' all slam an imaginary door, closing one arm over the chest.
4. Sleepily mime yawns and climbing stairs, slowing down throughout the last verse.

Extension 1
Add untuned percussion instruments to the running and yawning verses.
1. Give each child an instrument from a selection of tambourines, shakers and drums.
2. Play Running from the bears.
3. Say the chant. During the first three verses the instruments are placed on the floor, while the children perform the actions.
4. When the bears come home, the children tap or shake the instruments very quickly from 'I jumped' until 'HOUSE' when all stop.

Running from the bears

In this game, the children practise starting and stopping playing at a given signal. You will need enlarged photocopies of the start and stop cards opposite.

1. Give each child a small untuned percussion instrument. (Small home-made plastic pot shakers with lentil or rice filling are good for small hands to control.)
2. Choose a Goldilocks to conduct the other children with the start and stop cards.
3. The children hold their instruments still until Goldilocks shows the start card. Then they should play, stopping immediately on the stop card.

Extension 1 (continued)
5. During the last verse, in which the chant gets slower and slower, the children play their instruments again, matching the speed of their playing to the speed of the chanting.

Extension 2
1. Play Can't catch me.

2. Perform the whole chant with the new actions for the first three verses and the instrumental accompaniment for the last two.

Extension 3
Play Which bear? The actions from Extension 2 corresponds with the xylophone notes used in the game.

Can't catch me

The children learn a new verse and perform actions which establish a physical sense of low, medium and high. Perform the actions freely during the appropriate lines, as indicated below.

tap knees   tap chest   tap head

I don't like running from a great big bear,

A great big bear, a great big bear.

I don't like running from a middle-sized bear.

The small one can't catch me.

Which bear?

This game familiarises the children with the sound of low, medium and high pitches. They will need to have learned the actions from Can't catch me.

You will need a xylophone with note-bars C G and C'. First compare the length of the bars, noting that the longest bar makes the lowest sound, and the smallest makes the highest sound.

1. Repeat the new version of the chant and play this accompaniment to it, while the children perform the actions:

2. When the children are familiar with the sound for each bear, play this game. (To begin with the xylophone may be in full view. Later you may wish to hide it so that the children are recognising the pitches by listening alone.)

Play one of the note-bars and ask the children to show you which bear it belongs to by tapping their knees, chest or head.

3. A confident child may be asked to play the note-bars for the others to guess the bear.

C	C	C	C	C	C	C	C
I	don't	like	running	from a	great	big	bear,

C	C	C	C	C	C	C	C
A	great	big	bear,	a great	big	bear.	

G	G	G	G	G	G	G	G
I	don't	like running	from	a	middle-sized	bear.	

C'	C'	C'	C'	C'
The	small one	can't	catch	me.

Use hand signs for stop.

The magical musical box

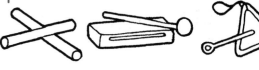

The children act out this story, playing the instruments in turn, collecting their sounds in the magical musical box, and learning to control volume. The song is sung to the tune of 'Hickory dickory dock'.

Part one

The king loved music. He listened to it all the time. All day long, the court musicians followed him round the palace, playing their instruments.

The trouble was, he liked to listen in bed, before he went to sleep. But he only had a very little bedroom and all the musicians couldn't fit in. And it wouldn't be fair to choose just one sort of instrument. Besides, he liked them all. He loved it when the shakers shook:

(SHAKERS SHAKE)

But he had to wave his arms and shout to make them stop.

(Wave arms and call, 'stop'.)

And he loved it when the scrapers scraped:

(SCRAPERS SCRAPE)

(Wave arms and call, 'stop'.)

And he definitely liked it when the tappers tapped:

(TAPPERS TAP)

(Wave arms and call, 'stop'.)

Best of all, he liked it when they all played together – although sometimes it got a bit noisy!

(EVERYONE PLAY)

'Stop!' shouted the king, waving his arms.

Part two

One day, the king was given a magical musical box. But the box was empty – it needed to be filled up with sounds. So, the king gathered all his musicians together.

'I'm going to collect all your sounds in my box,' he said. 'But you'll have to be patient and take your turn.'

The king lifted the lid of his magical musical box and carried it to each group of musicians in turn, singing this song as he collected their sounds.

Magical musical box!
Magical musical box!
It comes around,
You make the sound, (SHAKE)
Magical musical box!

When the king had collected all of the sounds, he went to his little bedroom, taking the box with him. He got into bed and snuggled down between the sheets. Then he reached out his hand and slowly opened the lid of the box just a little. *use hands close together*

(VERY QUIET MUSIC PLAYS)

And when he had listened for a while, he shut the lid and the music stopped.

(SHUT LID AND ALL STOP)

The king was happy. Now he could listen to a lovely mixture of instruments when he went to bed. The sound wasn't too loud - after all, it was night time and he didn't want to wake anyone up - it was just right.

He smiled to himself and fell fast asleep. And all that could be heard was happy snoring.

The magical musical box – activities

First things first
Tell the children the story, encouraging them to join you in making the sounds of the instruments with their voices. When you sing the song, pause at the end of the line 'you make the sound', in order to make 'shake', 'scrape', or 'tap' sounds.

Extension 1 – Part one
Prepare the children to participate in the story with percussion instruments. You will need three sets of instruments:

What is the sound in the box?

Name it and how it's played.

Play this game to develop the children's recognition and memory of the types and sounds of percussion instruments. You will need the musical box and an instrument from each of the three sets opposite.

1. Sit the children in a circle.
2. Play and identify the instruments according to whether they are shaken, tapped or scraped.
3. Place the instruments inside the box.
4. Choose a king.
5. Everyone sings this version of the song:

>   Magical musical box!
>   Magical musical box!
>   The king will play,
>   And we shall say,
>   What is the sound in the box.

6. The king chooses an instrument and shakes, scrapes or taps it inside the box. The others to say how it was played.

You will also need a magical musical box. This may be a decorated cardboard box with a hinged lid.

1. Play What is the sound in the box?
2. Organise the children into three groups, and allocate a set of instruments to each.
3. Choose one child to be the king.
4. Tell the first part of the story. As each sound is mentioned, the appropriate group plays, stopping when the king waves and calls 'stop'.

tappers

Lift the lid   Use hand signs.

clap then instruments
Take it in turns to be the king.

Play this game to develop the children's ability to control volume – first with clapping then with instruments. You will need the musical box.

1. Choose a king.
2. The king holds the musical box where everyone can see it.
3. As the king slowly raises the lid of the box, the other children start to clap very quietly then gradually louder. When the lid is fully open, the clapping is at its loudest; as the lid is lowered the clapping gets quieter; when the lid is closed the clapping stops.
4. Let other children be king.
5. Give everyone a percussion instrument, and play the game again.

Extension 2 – Part two

The sounds are 'collected' in the magical musical box, then the children learn to control the volume of their playing for the last part of the story – the scene in the king's bedroom. You will need the musical box and percussion instruments for three groups of players again.

1. Choose a king.
2. Everyone sings the song, pausing at the end of the penultimate line to collect one of the sounds. The king approaches the named group, opens the box, and closes it again when the group has played.
3. Play Lift the lid.
4. Tell part two of the story, incorporating the playing as rehearsed above.

Extension 3

Tell the whole story with the king and the instrumentalists acting out –
  • the sounds introduced in turn
  • collecting the sounds in the box
  • playing very quietly before the king sleeps.

Squintum's

In this story there are animal sounds and chants to join in with, and a song sung to the tune of 'In and out the dusky bluebells'.

Foxy was digging behind a stump and found a bumble bee. He put the bee in a bag and he travelled on.

(TRAVELLING SOUNDS)

At the first house he came to, he sang to the woman who lived there.

**Can I leave my bag here, lady,
Can I leave my bag here, lady,
Can I leave my bag here, lady,
While I go to Squintum's?**

And the woman sang back:

**You can leave your bag here, Foxy,
You can leave your bag here, Foxy,
You can leave your bag here, Foxy,
While you go to Squintum's.**

And foxy said:

**Don't be nosy, don't you peek,
I'll be back within the week.**

But as soon as Foxy was out of sight, the woman said:

I wonder what's in that bag?

And the minute the bag was opened, out flew the bumble bee!

Bzzzzzzzzzzzzzz!

And the rooster caught him and ate him up.

When Foxy came back, he took his bag and saw that his bee was gone. He shouted:

Where is my bee?

And the woman said:

**The bee's gone, the bee's gone,
The rooster ate the bee!**

'I'll have the rooster, then,' said Foxy. And he put the rooster in his bag and travelled on again.

(TRAVELLING SOUNDS)

At the second house he came to, he sang to the man who lived there:

**Can I leave my bag here, mister,
Can I leave my bag here, mister,
Can I leave my bag here, mister,
While I go to Squintum's?**

And the man sang back:

**You can leave your bag here, Foxy,
You can leave your bag here, Foxy,
You can leave your bag here, Foxy,
While you go to Squintum's.**

And Foxy said:

**Don't be nosy, don't you peek,
I'll be back within the week.**

But as soon as Foxy was out of sight, the man said:

I wonder what's in that bag?

And the minute the bag was opened, the rooster came squawking out!

Cock-a-doodle-doo!

And he got squished as flat as a pancake by the pig!

When Foxy came back, he saw that his rooster was gone. He shouted:

Where is my rooster?

And the man said:

**The rooster's gone, the rooster's gone,
The pig squished the rooster!**

'I'll have the pig, then,' said Foxy. And he put the pig in his bag and travelled on.

(TRAVELLING SOUNDS)

At the third house he came to, he sang to the woman who lived there:

Can I leave my bag here, lady ...

And the woman sang back:

You can leave your bag here, Foxy ...

And Foxy said:

Don't be nosy, don't you peek …

But as soon as he rounded the corner, the woman said:

I wonder what's in that bag?

And the minute the bag was opened, out came the pig!

Oink! Oink!

And he got tossed into an oak tree by the bull!

When Foxy came back, he saw that his pig was gone. He shouted:

Where is my pig?

And the woman said:

**The pig's gone, the pig's gone,
The bull tossed the pig!**

'I'll have the bull, then,' said Foxy. And he put the bull in his bag and travelled on again.

(TRAVELLING SOUNDS)

At the fourth house he came to, he sang to the man who lived there:

Can I leave my bag here, mister …

And the man sang back:

You can leave your bag here, Foxy …

And Foxy said:

Don't be nosy, don't you peek …

But as soon as Foxy was out of sight, the man said:

I wonder what's in that bag?

And the minute the bag was opened, the bull came out bellowing!

Mooooooo!

And he got chased away over the fields by the man's little servant boy!

When Foxy came back, he looked in his bag and shouted:

Where is my bull?

And the man said:

**The bull's gone, the bull's gone,
The boy chased the bull!**

'I'll have the boy, then,' said Foxy. And he put the boy in his bag and travelled on again.

(TRAVELLING SOUNDS)

At the fifth house he came to, he sang to the woman who lived there:

Can I leave my bag here, lady ...

And the woman sang back:

You can leave your bag here, Foxy ...

And Foxy said:

Don't be nosy, don't you peek ...

The woman was making cake and her children came around asking for some. They said:

Please, Mum, give me a piece!

The smell of the cake came to the little boy in the bag and he too said:

Please, Mum, give me a piece!

The woman opened the bag, and out jumped the little boy. Then into the bag she put the big, fierce, house dog. The little boy stopped crying and had some cake with the others.

After a while, Foxy came back. He took his bag, put it over his shoulder and travelled far into the deep woods.

(TRAVELLING SOUNDS)

Then he sat down and untied it. Out jumped the dog!

Woof! Woof! Woof!

Foxy ran for his life, with the big, fierce, house dog hot on his heels –

And he never did get to Squintum's!

Squintum's – activities

First things first
Tell the story. The children will quickly pick up the sung verses. Encourage them to join in with all the other chants and animal sounds.

Extension 1
Play Foxy's bag.

Extension 2
Retell the story. This time the children make the animal sounds on instruments.
1. First, discuss and select intsruments to represent each animal, eg

    bee: balloon and plastic blower (or simply release an inflated balloon)
    rooster: chime bars G and E
    pig: guiro
    bull: deep drum or gong
    boy in sack: voice (cup mouth with hands)
    dog: coconut shells

Experiment with the sounds: you might make a long sound for the bee, and two short sounds for the pig. Add the sound at the appropriate point in the story. (You will need to decide whether to use six groups of children or six soloists.)

2. Whenever the cue for travelling sounds occurs in the story, the children can tap their feet quietly but quickly on the floor, while one child plays 'trit trot' on a two-tone wood block:

Foxy's bag

Play this game when the children are familiar with the characters in the story. You will need to make enlarged card copies of the six character templates opposite. You will also need a cloth bag.

1. The children sit in a circle. Choose a child to be Foxy. Foxy secretly puts one of the shapes in the cloth bag, places it in front of one of the children in the circle, then walks around the circle saying:

> Don't be nosy, don't you peek,
> I'll be back within the week!

2. At the end of the chant, everyone says:

> I wonder what's in that bag.

The child with the bag then feels the shape without looking and makes the appropriate vocal sound for it, eg

> Oink! Oink!

3. The other children identify the animal by calling out together:

> The pig's out, the pig's out,
> The pig's out of the bag.

4. The child with the bag becomes Foxy and the game begins again, continuing until all the animals are out.

The big blue jeep and the little white trike

This eventful story is full of sound effects and short chants.

The big blue jeep and the little white trike stood at the traffic lights. The big blue jeep revved his engine and honked his horn impatiently.

Brmmm! Brmmm! Beep! Beep! Beep!

The little white trike didn't have an engine, so he tinkled his bell, just to say hello.

Tinkle, tinkle!

'Ha!' scoffed the big blue jeep. 'That's a silly little noise. Why don't you rev up your engine and honk your horn?'

'I don't have an engine or a horn,' explained the little white trike. 'Just pedals. And a bell.'

'No engine? How slow you must be.'

'I might be slow,' said the little white trike. 'But I get there in the end.'

'Oh yes?' sneered the big blue jeep. 'Not before me, though. Wheee! The lights are changing! Race you across town!'

And off he screeched in a big cloud of dust, shouting:

**Brmmm! Brmmm! Beep! Beep! Beep!
Can't catch me, I'm a big blue jeep!**

The little white trike waited until the light was green, then slowly pedalled off.

**Take it steady, take it slow,
Ring my bell and on I go.**

The big blue jeep zoomed round the

corner and skidded into a puddle with a screech of brakes.

Eeeeeee! Splash!

Oops. Muddy water, all over his nice, clean body work.

'Yuck!' said the big blue jeep. 'Can't have that. Time for the car wash.' And he revved his engines and zoomed off to the car wash, shouting:

Brmmm! Brmmm! Beep! Beep! Beep! Can't catch me, I'm a big blue jeep!

As he sat there enjoying the warm, soapy spray, he heard a little noise.

Tinkle, tinkle.

And the little white trike slowly pedalled by.

Take it steady, take it slow, Ring my bell and on I go.

When the big blue jeep was all clean again, he revved his engine and raced off, shouting:

Brmmm! Brmmm! ...

He went so fast, he felt really thirsty, and he started to cough and gasp.

Uh uh uh uh! Urrrrrrgh!

'Got to have a drink!' he groaned, and screeched to a halt by a petrol station. There, he had a long, long drink of petrol. While he was filling himself up, he heard a little noise.

Tinkle, tinkle.

And the little white trike slowly pedalled by.

Take it steady ...

When the big blue jeep finished his drink, he tore off again at top speed, shouting:

Brmmm! Brmmm! ...

There was a sharp nail lying on the road. The big blue jeep didn't see it in time.

BANG!

37

'Oh bother!' fumed the big blue jeep. 'A busted tyre! I'll have to go to a garage and get my spare put on.'

While he was sitting impatiently in the garage, waiting for his spare tyre to be put on, he heard a little noise.

Tinkle, tinkle.

And the little white trike slowly pedalled by.

Take it steady …

Changing the tyre took a long time. When the big blue jeep finally set off again, he went as fast as fast can be. He didn't stop at traffic lights or zebra crossings. He didn't look right or left at crossroads. He revved up his engine and he whooshed!

At last, he skidded to a halt on the other side of town. He was hot. His tyres hurt. He needed oil, water and a nice, long rest. But at least he had won the race. Or had he?

As he sat there exhausted, with steam rising from his over-heated bonnet, he heard a little noise.

Tinkle, tinkle.

And there, by the side of the road, was the little white trike. He was parked under a lamp post with his brakes on.

'That was fun,' said the little white trike. 'Let's do it again some time.'

And he let off his brake, looked both ways to make sure there was nothing coming, then slowly and steadily pedalled back down the road towards home.

Tinkle, tinkle …

The big blue jeep and the little white trike – activities

First things first
Tell the story, encouraging the children to join in with vocal sounds – the jeep's engine, the trike's bell, and so on.

Extension 1
Retell the story when you have talked about and chosen instrumental sounds to add to or replace the vocal sounds. Here are some ideas:
1. Find a bell sound to play each time the trike's 'tinkle tinkle' is mentioned.
2. Find sounds to describe the events which delay the jeep, eg

puddle splash	cymbal
empty tank cough	scraper
burst tyre	drum

Extension 2
1. Play Jeep trouble.
2. Find instrumental sounds for the car wash, filling the petrol, and replacing the tyre.
3. Appoint children to play instrumental sounds for the splash and the car wash, the empty tank and filling the petrol, bursting the tyre and replacing it. Appoint one child to play the trike's bell. All the other children make jeep noises.
4. 'Tell' the story in vocal and instrumental sounds. Use the go card to direct the jeep group. The trike plays throughout, stopping after the third set of breakdown sounds.
5. Make up a new set of obstacles for the jeep. Draw a map of the new journey and tell the story in sound, as above.

Jeep trouble

The children use their voices to make a sequence of sounds like a journey. You will need enlarged photocopies of the cards.

1. All practise the sound for each card.
2. Keeping the go card yourself, give the other three cards face down to three children. They look at the cards but keep them secret from the others.
3. Direct the main group with the go card. When you raise the go card, the children make engine sounds; when you lower it they stop. Point to one of the other three children during each gap. They make the appropriate sound for their card. Finish with the go card. The main group have to say in which order the events of the journey occurred.

GO	WASH	GARAGE	PETROL

brrrm brrrrm	swish swash	click clack	glug glug

Chicken Licken

The children join in with the chants and add actions for each character in this cumulative story, which lends itself to exploring vocal and instrumental texture.

 Chicken Licken was scratching in her yard when an acorn fell out of a tree and hit her on the head. She gave a loud squawk and said:

**Oh, my! Been hit by the sky!
The sky is falling down!
I gotta be quick,
I gotta be quick,
I got to tell the king!**

Along she went until she met Henny Penny.

Henny Penny said, 'Hello there, Chicken Licken. What's happening?'

Chicken Licken said:

Oh, my! Been hit by the sky ...

Henny Penny said,

I'd better come with you.

Along they went until they met Cocky Locky.

Cocky Locky said, 'Hello there, Henny Penny and Chicken Licken. What's happening?'

And the two of them said:

Oh, my! Been hit by the sky ...

Cocky Locky said,

I'd better come with you.

Along they went until they met Ducky Daddles.

Ducky Daddles said, 'Hello there, Cocky Locky, Henny Penny and Chicken Licken. What's happening?'

And the three of them said:

Oh, my! Been hit by the sky ...

Ducky Daddles said,

I'd better come with you.

Along they went until they met Goosey Loosey.

Goosey Loosey said, 'Hello there, Ducky Daddles, Cocky Locky, Henny Penny and Chicken Licken. What's happening?'

And the four of them said:

Oh, my! Been hit by the sky ...

Goosey Loosey said,

I'd better come with you.

Along they went until they met Turkey Lurkey.

Turkey Lurkey said, 'Hello there, Goosey Loosey, Ducky Daddles, Cocky Locky, Henny Penny and Chicken Licken. What's happening?'

And the five of them said:

Oh, my! Been hit by the sky ...

Turkey Lurkey said,

I'd better come with you.

Along they went until they met Foxy Woxy.

Foxy Woxy said, 'Hello there, Turkey Lurkey, Goosey Loosey, Ducky Daddles, Cocky Locky, Henny Penny and Chicken Licken. What's happening?'

And the six of them said:

Oh, my! Been hit by the sky ...

Foxy Woxy said, 'Then we will run to my den. I've got a phone there. Follow me, everyone!'

So, was the king ever told that the sky was falling down? What do you think?

Chicken Licken – activities

First things first
Tell the story with these actions:

 Chicken Licken – scrape the floor with one foot

 Henny Penny – bend knees up and down

 Cocky Locky – bend elbows and flap arms in and out

 Ducky Daddles – paddle hands alternately

 Goosey Loosey – nod chin up and down

 Turkey Lurkey – move head forwards and backwards

Extension 1
Tell the story again, but this time perform the chant and actions in groups.
1. Divide into six groups: one for each bird.
2. Make sure that everyone knows Chicken Licken's chant very well, and practise saying it like this: repeat the chant six times, starting with the Chicken Licken group and adding another group each time in the order they appear in the story. Once in, each group keeps repeating the chant. (The cumulative effect of each group joining in makes a crescendo – the sound gets louder.)

3. Repeat stage 2, but this time each group performs its action as well as saying the chant.
4. Tell the story. The groups join in in the correct order and keep their actions going right through to the end. The actions accumulate from a single into a six-part visual texture.

Extension 2
This time the texture and increase in loudness are achieved by playing instruments in groups.

1. Select a different type of instrument for each group to play, eg

   Chicken Licken – sandpaper blocks.

   Henny Penny – two tone woodblock.

   Cocky Locky – tear up newspaper strips of 3x20 cm. Tie them in the middle, fold, then tie the fold.

   Ducky Daddles – plastic bottles quarter filled with water, sloshed from side to side.

   Goosey Loosey – guiro.

   Turkey Lurkey – party blowers.

2. Play Farmyard band.
3. Tell the story with the instruments joining in one after the other, or cumulatively.

Farmyard band

The children play their bird names on instruments and explore textures. They work in the groups organised for extensions 1 and 2.

1. Choose one child from each group to conduct. When the conductor starts the group's action, the group responds by chanting its own name over and over, eg

   Henny Penny, Henny Penny …

Allow each conductor time to practise starting and stopping his or her group.
2. Give each group the instruments selected in extension 2. Now each group plays its own name on the instruments:

Hen - ny   Pen - ny   Hen - ny …

3. When the groups can confidently play their own names, select two or three of the conductors to combine their groups. Listen to the effect of the different combinations.
4. Next, the conductors bring in all six groups one after the other in the order of the story.
5. Appoint a fox (a child holding a glove-puppet) who hides behind a screen. Each time the fox appears, everyone must stop playing and 'freeze'.

The green wide-mouthed tree frog

The children make their mouths as wide as possible when they join in with the frog's chants. Later the children play with the rhythms of the food words – bananas, fruit and nuts, etc. They say the word rhythms first, then transfer them to instruments, acting out the story with the added sounds.

The green wide-mouthed tree frog went hopping through the rainforest. He wanted everyone to know who he was. He opened his wide mouth, and he said, very importantly:

**I'm a greeeeeeeen frog,
I'm a treeeeeeee frog,
I'm the greeeeenest greeeeen
You have ever seeeeen,
I'm a greeeeen wide-mouthed
Treeeeeeee frog!**

Before long, he came across a monkey hanging by its tail from a tree. The green wide-mouthed tree frog said:

**Cooooeeeee! Monkey!
I can seeeeeeee you!
What do you eeeeeat?**

The monkey said:

Bananas! Bananas!

And the green wide-mouthed tree frog said:

Deeeeeeeelicious!

And he hopped off, saying:

I'm a greeeeeeeen frog ...

A little later, he came across a brightly-coloured parrot. The green wide-mouthed tree frog said:

**Cooooeeeee! Parrot!
I can seeeeeeee you!
What do you eeeeeat?**

And the parrot said:

Fruit and nuts! Fruit and nuts!

And the green wide-mouthed tree frog said:

Deeeeeeeelicious!

And he hopped off, saying:

I'm a greeeeeeeen frog ...

Next, he came upon an armadillo, snuffling along the ground. The green wide-mouthed tree frog said:

**Cooooeeeee! Armadillo!
I can seeeeeeee you!
What do you eeeeeat?**

The armadillo said:

Termites! Termites!

And the green wide-mouthed tree frog said:

Deeeeeeeelicious!

And he hopped off, saying:

I'm a greeeeeeeen frog ...

He came upon the snake unexpectedly. It was sunning itself on a rock. It was a long, yellow one with red spots. The green wide-mouthed tree frog said:

**Cooooeeeee! Snake!
I can seeeeeeee you!
What do you eeeeeat?**

And the snake said:

Green wide-mouthed tree frogsss!

And the green wide-mouthed tree frog's big wide mouth closed up and got very tiny indeed. And he said in a small, small voice:

Ooh. Thatsh intereshting.

And very quietly, he tiptoed away.

The green wide-mouthed tree frog - activities

First things first
1. Tell the story encouraging the children to join in with the chants. Exaggerate the wide-mouthed ee sound.
2. Add actions for each animal, eg

   frog – hop on the spot
   monkey – hang by arm from tree
   parrot – flap wings
   armadillo – slow pawing and snuffling
   snake – slithering arm movement

Extension 1
1. Chant the food words. Then, all together, practise clapping the rhythms, eg

Ba - na - nas!   Ba - na - nas

Bananas! Bananas!

2. Divide into four small groups, one for each food. Each group chooses an instrument for its food, eg drum for bananas, maracas for fruit and nuts. Direct each group in turn to play its food rhythm.
3. Choose a child to act the part of the frog. Perform the story with each group playing its food rhythm at the appropriate place.

Fruit and nuts! Fruit and nuts

Termites! Termites!

Green wide-mouthed tree frogs!

Extension 2
1. Play What do you eat?
2. Develop the story further. Ask the children to think of more animals and their food rhythms. Practise playing them as a group or individually. Retell the story, adding your new animals.

What do you eat?

Play this peekaboo game to encourage children to choose and investigate food rhythms.

1. The children 'hide' by placing their hands over their eyes. You chant:

> Cooeee, Amy,
> I can see you!
> (Amy uncovers her eyes)
> What do you eat?

Amy replies: Beans on toast

2. You repeat the food while clapping the rhythm.

Beans   on toast.

3. Everyone uncovers their eyes to repeat the food while clapping the rhythm.

All:

Beans   on toast

4. Everyone covers their eyes again, and the game is repeated with another child.

Please, Mr Noah

This rap features animal sounds and actions which can be transferred onto instruments to accompany the story.

Part one – Into the ark

Please, Mr Noah,
The sky's gone dark!
May we come
Into your ark?

I've gotta say yes,
I can't say no,
Just make your sound and
In you go.

Where are the snakes?
Sssssssssssss,
Well done, snakes, and
In you go!

Where are the crocodiles?
Snip snap, snip snap,
Well done, crocodiles, and
In you go!

Where are the rabbits?
Hop and stop, hop and stop,
Well done, rabbits, and
In you go!

Where are the lions?
Roar, roar!
Well done, lions, and
In you go!

Where are the monkeys?
Chitter chatter, chitter chatter,
Well done, monkeys, and
In you go!

Where are the elephants?
Stomp along,
Well done, elephants, and
In you go!

The rain came down,
And the sky was dark,
But Noah and the animals
Were safe in the ark.

Part two – Inside the ark

Inside the ark
It was dark and hot.
Were they quiet?
They were not!

The snakes got cross,
Sssssssssss!
The crocodiles were bored,
Snip snap snip snap!
The rabbits got restless,
Hop and stop, hop and stop.
The lions just roared,
Roar! Roar!
The monkeys went bananas,
Chitter chatter chitter chatter.
Elephants, too,
Stomp along,
Noah got a headache,
Ooooh, my head!
What was he to do?
Order, order!

STOP! said Noah!
Stop, stop, stop!
I think I see
A mountain top!

HOORAY!

Please, Mr Noah – activities

First things first
Chant the story to the children to familiarise them with it.

Extension 1 – Into the ark
1. Divide the children into six animal groups.
2. Allow each group practice at saying its sound. Do this rhythmically: tap four beats on a tambour and say each sound to the beat (before each sound, count and tap four beats to bring all the children in together):

(1 2 3 4)	1	2	3	4
snakes	sssssssssssssssssssssssssssssss			
crocodiles	snip	snap	snip	snap
rabbits	hop and stop		hop and stop	
lions	roar		roar	
monkeys	chit-ter	chat-ter	chit-ter	chat-ter
elephants	stomp	a	-	long

3. Ask the children to devise a movement which matches the sound pattern for their animal, eg the rabbit group might wag hands like ears in time to 'hop and stop'.
4. Chant the story again. Each group joins in with its animal words and actions at the appropriate line, eg

(1 2 3 4)	1	2	3	4
snakes	Where are the snakes? sssssssssssssssssssssssssssssss Well done snakes and In you go!			

Extension 2 – Inside the ark
The children make the same vocal sounds and movements as before. This time, instead of saying the sound just once, they repeat it until all are ordered to stop by Noah.
1. Play Animal crackers.
2. Organise the children into six groups again and warn them to be ready to make their vocal animal sounds.
3. Chant the second part of the story. Nod to each animal group in turn to join in at the appropriate line, then keep going.

Extension 3
Tell the whole Noah story again. This time the children make the animal sounds on the instruments suggested below. They play only on the appropriate line during part one, and in part two, they continue to play until the signal to stop.

50

Animal crackers

The children practise vocal control in stopping and starting the animal sounds, then transfer the activity to instruments. Enlarge a copy of the chart below.

1. As you point to each animal, one after the other, all the children make its sound. Appoint a confident child to tap the steady count of four beats over and over again on a tambour.

2. Divide the children into the six animal groups. When the group's animal is pointed to, the group makes its sound and continues until all six groups have joined in.

3. Repeat the game from the beginning using the instruments in extension 3.

Animal crackers – chart

	1	2	3	4	
🐍	sssssssssssssssssssssssssssssssssssssssssssssssssssssssss				
🐊	snip	snap	snip	snap	
🐰	hop and stop		hop and stop		
🦁	roar		roar		
🐒	chit - ter	chat - ter	chit - ter	chat - ter	
🐘	stomp	a	-	long	

51

The aliens

In this story, which includes a game, the children make sound effects with their voices for the spaceship, and talk to each other in alien language by making up and copying nonsense words. The game may be extended into instrumental conversations.

One dark night, there was a strange, humming sound coming from the sky!

(QUIET AND LOW VOCAL HUM)

First, it was very quiet. Then it got louder ... and louder ... and louder.

(HUMMING GETS LOUDER)

And over the trees, there appeared a big, round, silver spaceship! It hovered for a moment – then, slowly, it came down and landed with a bump.

(TAP KNEES.)

For a little while nothing happened. Then a door slid open with a hissing sound ...

(SHORT VOCAL HISS)

... and a ramp came down.

(GLOCKENSPIEL – PING, PING, PING ...)

The aliens wore round helmets. Slowly, they walked down the ramp ...

(CLICK TONGUES)

... and the ramp closed behind them.

(GLOCKENSPIEL – TRING)

The aliens sat in a circle. One of them had a strange, cone-shaped object. This was passed around the circle. As it moved around, the aliens began to chant.

**Oomi goomi ding dong,
Ooomi goomi goo,
Woogalum, googalum,
Wotsay yoo?**

As soon as the chant finished, the alien who was holding the strange cone said this (child makes up alien sentence, eg):

Oomi goomi oomi goomi.

The other aliens immediately echoed.

Oomi goomi oomi goomi.

(PING, PING, PING ...)

The ramp came down again, and the aliens walked back up into the spaceship.

(CLICK TONGUES)

The ramp folded up behind them ...

(TRING)

... and the doors closed.

(SHORT HISS)

The engines began to hum quietly ...

(QUIET AND LOW HUM)

... then louder ...

(HUMMING GETS LOUDER)

... and the spaceship took off.

(HUMMING GETS LOUDER AND HIGHER)

It flew away over the trees ...

(HUMMING GETS QUIETER)

... and was never seen again.

(SILENCE)

I wonder what they were talking about?

The aliens – activities

First things first
1. Talk about imaginary aliens. How might they speak? Play Alien echoes.

Alien echoes

You will need a small glockenspiel, the 'ramp', and a cardboard 'megaphone', preferably sprayed silver or covered in foil.

1. Sit the children in a circle.
2. Signal the start of the game by playing the glockenspiel ramp sounds. Play all the note-bars from top to bottom (short to long) – PING PING PING … Close the ramp by running the beaters quickly back up from bottom to top – TRING.
3. The children pass the megaphone around the circle while they chant:

> Oomi goomi ding dong,
> Oomi goomi goo,
> Woogalum, googalum
> Wotsay you?

4. At the end of the chant, the child holding the megaphone says something in alien language. The other children immediately copy what was said.
5. Repeat the as many times as you want, then signal the end of the game with the ramp sound.

2. Tell the story. You will need the megaphone and glockenspiel for the game.
3. Encourage the children to join in with the vocal spaceship sounds – the humming, hissing, tongue clicking, and so on.
3. Insert the game at the appropriate place, then continue the story.

Extension 1
Make a small model spaceship out of junk materials and together practise ways of creating vocal or instrumental sounds for the engine, the door, the landing, and so on.

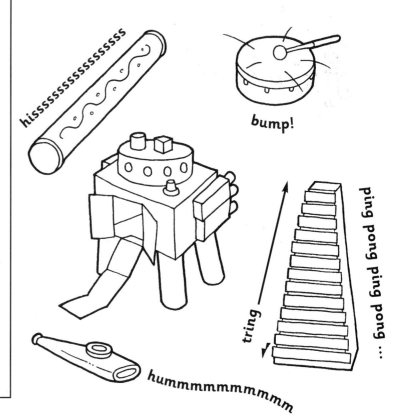

Alien conversations

In this version of the game, the children have conversations using pairs of percussion instruments, eg

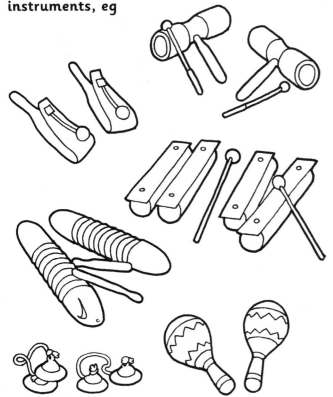

You will need enough pairs for every child to have an instrument.
1. Sit in a circle and place an instrument on the floor in front of each child.
2. Signal the start of the game with the glockenspiel as before.
3. Say the chant and pass the megaphone around the circle.
4. The child holding the megaphone at the end of the chant 'says' something on his or her instrument. The child with the matching instrument replies – saying something similar but slightly different. The conversation continues with each child taking turns to play.
5. Repeat the chant and conversations until everyone has had a turn. Remind the children to think about different ways in which they can use the instruments like voices having conversations – quietly, loudly, quickly, slowly, short sounds or long.
6. Signal the end of the game by playing the glockenspiel ramp sound.

Extension 2
Play Alien conversations.

Extension 3
1. Tell the story in sound and action only, using the vocal and instrumental sound ideas you worked on in extension 1.

2. Insert Alien conversations and use the instruments like voices having a conversation.

Cinderella

This story includes sound effects, and a song to the tune of 'London's burning'.

(Sing)
**Who arises with the sun?
Who arises with the sun?
So much work to be done,
Cinderella, Cinderella.**

Poor Cinderella. She worked so hard. She swept the floor.

brish   brish   brush

She chopped the wood for the fire.

chip   chip   chop

She polished the windows until they shone.

rub   rub   dub

And all day long, her nasty step-sisters shouted at her.
(Sing in a harsh, bossy way.)

**Cinderella, get the broom,
Cinderella, get the broom,
Hurry up, clean the room,
Cinderella, Cinderella.**

One day, an invitation arrived from the palace. The prince was going to have a ball. All the ladies in the land were invited. But Cinderella's mean sisters wouldn't let her go. She sat in the kitchen, crying.

drip   drip   drop

(Sing sadly)
**They have gone, there's only me,
They have gone, there's only me,
I'm as sad as can be,
Cinderella, Cinderella.**

And then something wonderful happened. A beautiful fairy with a magic wand appeared.

Some little mice changed into coachmen.

ma - gic wand

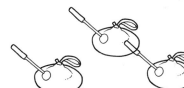

mice coach - men

She said, 'I am your fairy godmother.'

(Sing sweetly)
**Cinderella, don't be blue,
Cinderella, don't be blue,
Every wish will come true,
Cinderella, Cinderella.**

When she waved her wand, all kinds of amazing things happened. A pumpkin changed into a golden coach.

And, best of all, Cinderella's rags disappeared and she found she was wearing a beautiful dress and a pair of glass slippers.

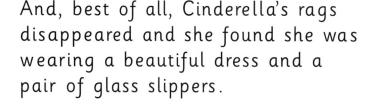

glass slip - pers

Cinderella was so happy. But the fairy godmother said, 'You must be home by midnight.'

gol - den coach

'I will,' said Cinderella. She got into the coach and drove away, singing:

**I'll be dancing at the ball,
I'll be dancing at the ball,
It's the best night of all,
Cinderella, Cinderella.**

Cinderella had a lovely time at the ball. The prince danced with her all evening. (Play the song accompaniment.) But then …

ding   ding   ding (x4)

… the clock struck twelve times for midnight. 'I must go,' said Cinderella, and she ran down the steps to her coach. But she left one of her glass slippers behind. The prince picked it up.

'Whoever fits this shoe will be my wife,' he said.

The next day, all the ladies in the land tried the slipper on. But it didn't fit. Cinderella's step-sisters tried too, but their feet were much too big. 'Does anyone else live here?' asked the prince.

'NO!' shouted the step-sisters.

'YES!' said Cinderella, coming in from the kitchen. 'I do. Can I try it on?'

She was back in her rags again, but the prince thought he recognised her.

'Please do,' he said.
So Cinderella tried on the slipper – and it fitted perfectly!

Hooray! (Sing joyfully, and play all the instruments.)

**They got married in the spring,
They got married in the spring,
Hear the bells, how they ring,
Cinderella, Cinderella.**

Cinderella – activities

First things first
Tell the story. Encourage the children to join in singing the verses of the song, changing their voices to suit the characters.

Extension 1
A steady count of three underpins the song and all the other sounds in the story. Establish a feeling for this by practising together the action pattern opposite.
1. Practise it first with the count (you count aloud and perform the actions, while the children just copy the actions). Then practise it without the count.

Count	1	2	3
Actions			

2. Now add the melody. While the children perform the action pattern over and over again, you sing the melody to 'la', then to the words. Some children may start to join you in singing the melody with or without the words. For many, it will be enough to perform the actions while listening to the melody.

Count	1	2	3	1	2	3
Actions						
Sing						When the
	day	has	just be - gun			Who a-
	ri -	ses	with the sun,			So much
	work		to be done,			Cin - de -
	-rel	-la	Cin - de - rel -	la.		

Extension 2

The additional sounds in the story also fit a pattern of three counts - the children now learn to play these on instruments. You will need the instruments suggested in the illustrations, or similar substitutes.

1. Divide into eight groups. Each group is given a turn to play its instruments while all the other children chant the appropriate words, eg

First group

All   brish brish brush
       brish brish brush
       brish brish brush ...

2. Appoint a fairy godmother to start and stop the sound with a wave of a pencil or ruler – her magic wand.
3. Give each group practice in playing its sound.

Extension 3

1. Add the instruments to the appropriate song verses. Some verses will have more than one group playing, eg the first verse may have all the cleaning sounds; the ball verse may have the magical coach, mice and slipper sounds.
2. Give each group practice in playing its sound while the others sing the verse. (The example below shows the 'drip drip drop' sound added to the crying verse.)
3. Appoint one child to play the midnight chimes on an F chime bar, and practise counting the chimes together.

Count	1	2	3	1	2	3
Play	🐭	🐭	🐭	🐭	🐭	🐭
Sing						They have
	gone	there's	only	me		They have
	gone	there's	only	me		I'm as
	sad		as can	be		Cin - de -
	-rel	-la	Cin - de - rel	- la.		

Extension 4

1. **Add the tuned percussion accompaniment below to the verses. You will need chime bars F A C, which correspond with the action pattern: F – low (knees), A – medium (chest), C – high (head). You or a confident child may play this, while the others sing.**
2. **Practise playing the tuned percussion accompaniment while some children sing the verses, and the groups take turns to add their instruments.**
3. **Make dance music for the ball by playing the tuned percussion accompaniment and adding the eight instrumental groups. You will need a fairy godmother to conduct again. When she points her wand to a group they join in, when she points to them again they stop.**
4. **Finally, tell the whole story. Each group plays its sound as cued then joins in when its verse is sung by the other children. The fairy godmother starts the ball music, conducting the groups to start or stop. When the midnight chimes are heard, everyone stops playing. All join in playing, singing or with actions for the final celebration verse.**

Count	1	2	3	1	2	3
Actions	knees	chest	head	knees	chest	head
Play	F	A	C	F	A	C
Sing						When the
	day	has	just be-gun			Who a-
	ri -	ses	with the sun,			So much
	work		to be done,			Cin - de -
	-rel	-la	Cin - de - rel -	la.		

Song melodies

Little Red Riding Hood

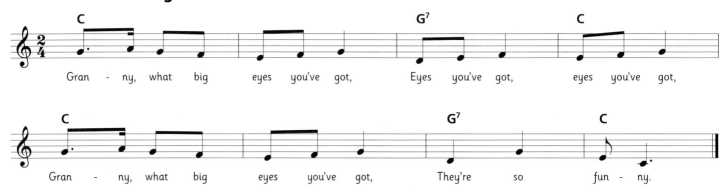

The meanest king   first song

The meanest king
second song

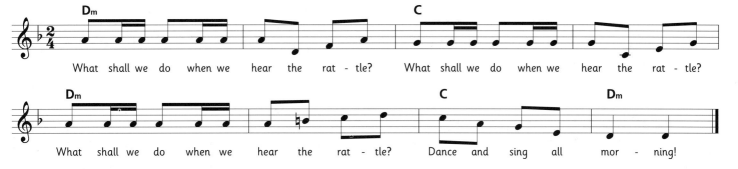

Pinocchio

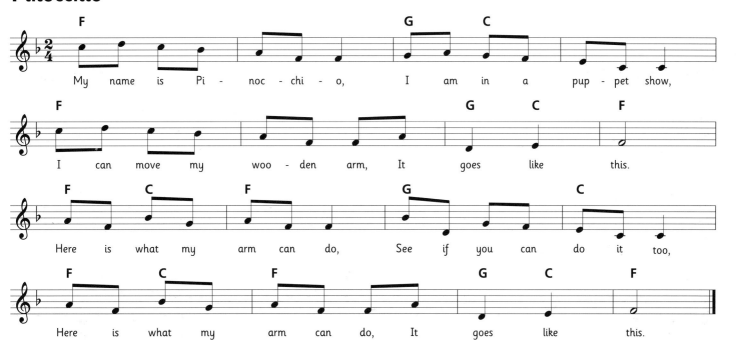

The magical musical box

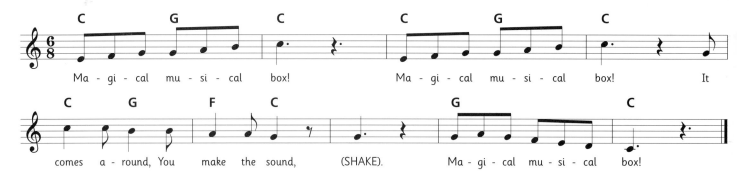

Squintum's

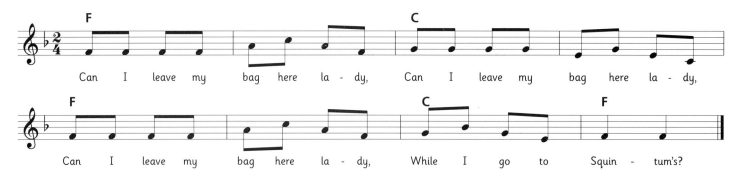

Cinderella

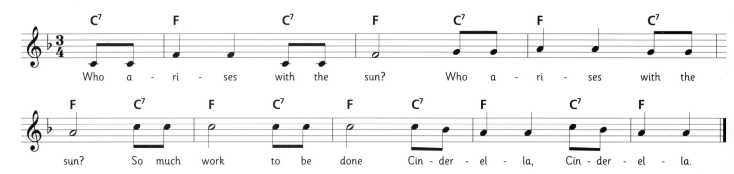